Contents

These Summary N analyse all 15 poe Conflict antholog Literature.

For each poem, you will find:

- Detailed line-by-line annotations and insightful analysis of poetic techniques
- Key biographical info about the poet
- A concise summary of the relevant literary and historical context
- A clear explanation of the poem’s meaning and authorial intent
- Colour-coded thematic ideas to highlight connections between poems

We hope this gives you a solid foundation to explore your own interpretations of these poems in your essays.

Happy reading!

💚 SnapRevise

'Bayonet Charge' by Ted Hughes

Key information

- **Poet:** Ted Hughes (1930–1998)
- **Year:** 1957
- **Form:** Blank verse, 3 stanzas
- **Key techniques:** Visceral imagery, beginning in media res, anthropomorphisation

About the poet

Ted Hughes was an influential English poet, known for stark portrayals of nature and visceral intensity. Born in Yorkshire, his early life was shaped by the austere landscapes of northern England and the trauma of WWII, which deeply informed his later work. His famous collection *The Hawk in the Rain* (1957) established his reputation, and his later role as Poet Laureate cemented his place in the British literary canon.

Historical context

Hughes was born in the interwar period and grew up during WWII. His father was a WWI veteran. In the 1950s, England was still recovering from the toll of WWII.

Literary context

This poem is a product of 20th century England and late Modernism. Hughes was also influenced by the works of Wilfred Owen, the WWI poet and author of some of the most famous pacifist/anti-war poetry such as 'Dulce et Decorum est.'

Summary

'Bayonet Charge' captures the horrors of war, depicting the psychological and physical disarray of a soldier in the midst of battle. It reflects an attitude of post-war disillusionment and explores the brutal, often senseless violence of war, mirroring the broader societal anxieties of the 20th century.

Through intense imagery and a focus on individual trauma, Hughes explores the personal cost of warfare and reveals the dehumanising forces at the heart of the conflict. The poem describes a WWI soldier running through no man's land armed with his bayonet. In the midst of the disorienting chaos, he almost stops to ponder "the reason / Of his still running" and the senselessness of war. He sees a rabbit die in the crossfire and keeps running with no regard for "King, honour, human dignity" – he is simply desperate to survive. By the end, even his fear is characterised as "dynamite" as he has been so dehumanised that every emotion has become a dangerous, destructive product of war.

Key ideas

- Internalisation of war
- Psychological experience of soldiers
- Futility of war
- Dehumanising impact of war
- Innocent and powerless victims of war
- The effect of war on nature and the environment

Beginning in media res with the adverb "suddenly" establishing surprise and urgency; the reader feels the same suddenness as the subject in the poem

Change of tense from past ("awoke") to present continuous ("was running") amplifies the sense of confusion, as though the subject must act without thinking

Repetition of "raw" and caesura separating "raw" at the end of the line emphasises the stark, visceral reality of war

Enjambment across the first stanza creates breathlessness and emulates the disorienting nature of active combat

Reoccurs in line 19 as a simple, natural symbol of safety and normalcy, evocative of a British garden

Suddenly he awoke and was running – raw
In raw-seamed hot khaki, his sweat heavy,
Stumbling across a field of clods towards a green hedge
That dazzled with rifle fire, hearing
Bullets smacking the belly out of the air –
He lugged a rifle numb as a smashed arm;
The patriotic tear that had brimmed in his eye
Sweating like molten iron from the centre of his chest, –

Anthropomorphising bullets, the air, and the rifle – indicative of the search for humanity amidst violent chaos

Kinaesthetic imagery and evocative sensory descriptions in the semantic field of a soldier's experience

Line 7 is a sentence fragment; there is no verb describing what the "patriotic tear" does, perhaps suggesting this sense of duty is purposeless.

Also "had brimmed" = past tense; he no longer has patriotic tears left to shed?

Likening the rifle to an arm, implying it is an integral part of a soldier's body even when he/it is numb and smashed

A visceral simile suggesting his own body is a danger to himself

Ambiguity/confusion – he is constantly running throughout the poem, but here he hesitates

In bewilderment then he almost stopped –
In what cold clockwork of the stars and the nations
Was he the hand pointing that second? He was running
Like a man who has jumped up in the dark and runs
Listening between his footfalls for the reason
Of his still running, and his foot hung like
Statuary in mid-stride. Then the shot-slashed furrows

Stars = fate, and Nations = opposing sides in the war; both grandiose terms for distant/abstract entities

Alliteration of c/k sounds in conveys his moral distaste for the war machine that sends men to die

He is metaphorically in the dark because he doesn't understand his own actions; could also be a metaphor for enlisting for war – "jump[ing] up in the dark" without truly understanding what he is jumping into

Repetition of running but still not knowing why, underscoring futility

Evokes imagery of statues of war heroes, but contrasts this patriotic symbol with the soldier's doubts and confusion

Threw up a yellow hare that rolled like a flame
And crawled in a threshing circle, its mouth wide
Open silent, its eyes standing out.
He plunged past with his bayonet toward the green hedge,
King, honour, human dignity, etcetera
Dropped like luxuries in a yelling alarm
To get out of that blue crackling air
His terror's touchy dynamite.

Simile that likens an innocent animal to a destructive force – almost like the hare evaporates into flames

Imagery of death, emptiness, a living creature reduced to a vacant shell

Implied to be a bastion of hope and safety

Anaphora/listing and the flippant tone of "etcetera" implies these abstract ideals have no relevance in reality – they are like "luxuries" you would drop when fleeing a disaster

Unnatural force of gunfire disrupting the environment like lightning – further imagery of danger

Theme key

- [red] = war
- [pink] = psychological conflict
- [green] = nature
- [blue] = futility

The poem ends without a sense of resolution; we know the soldier was going "toward the green hedge" but we don't know if he made it. Instead, Hughes concentrates on this isolated moment in the heat of battle where this one soldier's experience is a metonym for the horrors of war inflicted on all those who served.

Key information

- **Poet:** Alfred, Lord Tennyson (1809–1892)
- **Year:** 1854
- **Form:** Dactylic dimeter, ballad with 6 stanzas
- **Key techniques:** Repetition, personification, anaphora

About the poet

Alfred, Lord Tennyson was a British poet and was the longest serving Poet Laureate of the United Kingdom for over 40 years (from 1850 until his death in 1892). This position gave him a platform to write poems on national events and issues, and he often wrote deeply patriotic and sentimental works to reflect or shape public perception. He was heavily influenced by Romanticism in his efforts to capture the Victorian spirit and moral righteousness.

Historical context

The Charge of the Light Brigade was a military manoeuvre that took place during the Battle of Balaclava in the Crimean War (1853–1856) when 600 British soldiers were ordered to charge Russian artillery troops and only 247 men survived. This poem was written shortly after this event when it was still at the forefront of the public consciousness.

Literary context

Tennyson often wrote narrative poems with mythological elements to convey grandeur, heroism, and national spirit. Tennyson was the Poet Laureate throughout most of the Victorian era, making him an authoritative voice within the United Kingdom.

Summary

This poem is about soldiers’ bravery when confronted with certain death. With a vigorous and relentless rhythm, Tennyson conveys the rapid pace of a British Light Brigade marching towards their inevitable end. He describes how 600 soldiers were ordered to advance upon an artillery unit – orders which the soldiers followed unquestioningly, as was their duty. Even when the brigade is fired upon by cannons and guns, they march onwards into “Hell” and “Death,” putting up a valiant fight and breaking through enemy lines before falling back, though they sustain heavy casualties. The poem ends with an imperative call to always remember the glorious bravery of these soldiers. The poem reflects the Victorian ideal of duty and loyalty to one’s country and commanding officers, but it also subtly critiques the mistakes that led to the charge, suggesting that blind obedience to authority can have fatal consequences. Thus, Tennyson venerates the bravery of soldiers whilst simultaneously critiquing the industry of war that sends soldiers to their deaths; he honours the people but laments the circumstances that led to their sacrifice.

Key ideas

- Bravery in conflict
- Soldiers as individuals and a collective
- Futility of war
- Innocent and powerless victims of war
- Death, loss, and sacrifice
- Power of memory

Dactylic structure (one stressed syllable, two unstressed syllables) creates a falling rhythm that mimics galloping horses

Biblical allusion to Psalm 23 about having faith in God even when confronting doom

Introduction of a refrain to convey the ubiquity and inevitability of death

A solemn refrain and reminder of the spirit of sacrifice as well as the scale of death; the collective term "the six hundred" presents the cavalry as a unified force

Rhetorical question that implies no soldier questioned their orders or considered shirking their duty

Critique of military leadership, but no specific attribution of blame — all the soldiers know is that "someone" has made a mistake that will likely cost them their lives

Catalectic line that breaks the poem's normal dactylic meter, thereby emphasising the blunder and its disruption of the soldiers' lives

Anaphoric repetition making the cannons seem ubiquitous, trapping the soldiers

Sibilant 's' sounds are reminiscent of the whizzing artillery fire

I Half a league, half a league,
Half a league onward,
All in the valley of Death
Rode the six hundred.
"Forward, the Light Brigade!
Charge for the guns!" he said.
Into the valley of Death
Rode the six hundred.

II "Forward, the Light Brigade!"
Was there a man dismayed?
Not though the soldier knew
Someone had blundered.
Theirs not to make reply,
Theirs not to reason why,
Theirs but to do and die.
Into the valley of Death
Rode the six hundred.

III Cannon to right of them,
Cannon to left of them,
Cannon in front of them
Volleyed and thundered;
Stormed at with shot and shell,
Boldly they rode and well,
Into the jaws of Death,
Into the mouth of hell
Rode the six hundred.

League = 1 ½ miles, so troops cover a vast distance at fast pace, heightening tension

Direct speech creates present-tense immediacy

Pause at the end of the line before reiterating not all returned, forcing the reader to stop and dwell on the loss

Antithesis contrasting "do and die" with "reason why" highlights their unquestioning obedience, and the use of rhyme creates associations between death and duty

Earlier "valley of Death" becomes "jaws of Death and mouth of hell" — more menacing and diabolical

Assonant open vowel sounds in 'boldly,' 'rode,' 'jaws,' and 'mouth' create a sense of hollowness, subtly implying their efforts are in vain

IV Flashed all their sabres bare,
Flashed as they turned in air
Sabring the gunners there,
Charging an army, while
All the world wondered.
Plunged in the battery-smoke
Right through the line they broke;
Cossack and Russian
Reeled from the sabre stroke
Shattered and sundered.
Then they rode back, but not
Not the six hundred.

V Cannon to right of them,
Cannon to left of them,
Cannon behind them
Volleyed and thundered;
Stormed at with shot and shell,
While horse and hero fell.
They that had fought so well
Came through the jaws of Death,
Back from the mouth of hell,
All that was left of them,
Left of six hundred.

Numerically as well as psychologically

VI When can their glory fade?
O the wild charge they made!
All the world wondered.
Honour the charge they made!
Honour the Light Brigade,
Noble six hundred!

Imperative commands and directly imploring readers to respect and remember the spirit and sacrifice of this brigade

Militaristic imagery of weapons foreshadowing violence

Almost like the forces are frozen in time, poised for a grand battle painting that immortalises their bravery without showing the horrifying physicality or psychology of facing death

Brief aside to remind us of the astonishment or naivete of civilians back home

Conveys success, but then is undercut by the laconic line "not the six hundred," reinforcing that victory comes at a cost

Earlier cannons in front become cannons behind as the soldiers are under fire both when they approach and retreat — they are surrounded by danger, no direction is safe

Repeated personification of Death and hell as ravenous entities eager to devour

Sixth stanza for the six hundred celebrates their heroism, elevating them to the "noble" forces deserving of honour

Theme key

- = bravery in conflict
- = tension and death
- = duty and sacrifice
- = memory

‘Checking Out Me History’ by John Agard

SNAPREVISE

Key information

- **Poet:** John Agard (1949–)
- **Year:** 2004
- **Form:** Free verse
- **Key techniques:** Interpolation, allusions, juxtaposition

About the poet

John Agard is a renowned poet and author whose work reflects his Guyanese heritage and experiences living in Britain as of 1977. He gained recognition for his unique writing style, which blends Caribbean rhythms with sharp social commentary. His writing typically examines themes of identity, race, migration, marginalisation, and power.

Historical context

This poem critiques the Eurocentric focus of the British education system. Agard, who was born in Guyana, a nation that was under British colonial rule until 1966, meaning history lessons often prioritised European figures while ignoring key Black and Caribbean historical figures due to systemic bias. His poem reflects this frustration, highlighting important figures like Toussaint L’Ouverture and Mary Seacole left out of mainstream narratives.

Literary context

This poem belongs to the tradition of postcolonial literature which challenges Eurocentric narratives and gives voice to historically marginalised communities. Agard draws on British cultural touchstones as well as the oral storytelling traditions of the Caribbean, using rhythm, repetition, and phonetic Creole spelling to reflect Agard’s Guyanese heritage.

Summary

In this poem, Agard reflects on the way history is taught in schools where the focus is often on white European figures and events, while the contributions and history of Black people and Caribbean cultures are overlooked or distorted. He adopts a playful tone contrasting the traditional Eurocentric curriculum with the diverse stories of Black history. Through this, he compels readers to acknowledge the difference between ‘history’ as a school subject or agreed-upon perspective and ‘my history’ or personal, more inclusive reclamations of the past. The poem alternates between descriptions of colonial narratives framed with the repetition of “dem tell me,” highlighting the authoritative nature of what is taught, and italicised descriptions of what “dem never tell me” in which Agard highlights unsung heroes from Black history.

Key ideas

- Power governs perspective
- Experiences of the powerless
- Reclaiming power
- Subjectivity and bias
- Empowerment through language

Annotations

SNAPREVISE

Dem tell me
Dem tell me
Wha dem want to tell me

Bandage up me eye with me own history
Blind me to my own identity

Dem tell me bout 1066 and all dat
dem tell me bout Dick Whittington and he cat
But Touissant L'Ouverture
no dem never tell me bout dat

Toussaint a slave
with vision
lick back
Napoleon
battalion
and first Black
Republic born
Toussaint de thorn
to de French
Toussaint de beacon
of de Haitian Revolution

Dem tell me bout de man who discover de balloon
and de cow who jump over de moon
Dem tell me bout de dish run away with de spoon
but dem never tell me bout Nanny de maroon

Nanny
see-far woman
of mountain dream
fire-woman struggle
hopeful stream
to freedom river

Dem tell me bout Lord Nelson and Waterloo
but dem never tell me bout Shaka de great Zulu
Dem tell me bout Columbus and 1492
but what happen to de Caribs and de Arawaks too

Dem tell me bout Florence Nightingale and she lamp
and how Robin Hood used to camp
Dem tell me bout ole King Cole was a merry ole soul
but dem never tell me bout Mary Seacole

From Jamaica
she travel far
to the Crimean War
she volunteer to go
and even when de British said no
she still brave the Russian snow
a healing star
among the wounded
a yellow sunrise
to the dying

Dem tell me
Dem tell me wha dem want to tell me
But now I checking out me own history
I carving out me identity

Annotations:

- Creole heightens the authenticity of the speaker's voice and cultural perspective, challenging the dominance of Standard English; also creates an 'us and them' or 'me and dem' dichotomy
- Repetition emphasises frustration and oppression, as though the speaker has been told over and over again
- Symbolic blindness to disempower and disconnect the speaker from his own culture and identity
- Introduces a power dynamic between dem who seek to control or manipulate the speaker's understanding of reality through presenting a selective history
- Juxtaposition of major historical events like the Battle of Hastings with trivial folklore like Dick Wittington undermines the legitimacy of dominant historical narratives (i.e. implies it is silly that Dick Wittington's cat is given more attention than the Haitian Revolution)
- Minimalist line structure (only 1-3 words per line) makes each phrase more emphatic, but also suggests fragmentation, like history is being pieced together
- Shift in structure and italicised stanza disrupts the colonial erasure by interjecting with the story of Toussaint, showing readers a vivid and inspiring example of Black history that had been ignored or suppressed
- Outlines the history of Toussaint's rebellion in just 9 words, further ridiculing the education system for not making time to teach this
- More trivialities and nursery rhymes in stark contrast to meaningful historical figures and moments; furthers the sense of injustice that vital knowledge is supplanted by childish rhymes
- Symbols of hope and guidance, hence learning about Toussaint and Seacole can offer hope for reclaiming power and independence
- Shift to personal empowerment; speaker is actively reclaiming what is theirs, implying they are righting an historical injustice and no longer being a passive recipient of what dem want to tell
- Connotes wisdom, foresight, and leadership – traits dem are trying to suppress or discourage
- Semantic field of optimism and hope, reinforcing the inspiring narratives in Black history
- Rhyming pairs of colonial history with Black history perhaps imply that these stories could be taught alongside each other, if dem would permit it
- Reminder of the absurdity of learning about fictional heroes at the expense of real ones
- Explicitly challenges the glorification of Columbus and colonialist practices that led to the genocide of indigenous populations by forcing readers to ponder "what happen[ed]" to these people
- Allusion to Seacole being rejected by the British army but accomplishing great feats regardless
- Carving connotes deep permanence and creation. Equating history with identity implies an intrinsic link between knowledge of the past and power in the present

Theme key

- Orange = cultural authenticity
- Pink = oppression
- Green = historical allusions
- Blue = empowerment

‘The Émigrée’ by Carol Rumens

SNAPREVISE

Key information

- **Poet:** Carol Rumens (1944–)
- **Year:** 1993
- **Form:** Free verse
- **Key techniques:** Nostalgia, personification, motif of light

About the poet

Carol Rumens is a British poet and writer who has had an impressive career in the literary world. Although she did not experience life as an émigrée herself (so it is important to separate Rumens’ authorial voice from the speaker’s voice), she often writes about universal themes like journeys, self-discovery, and a connection to place that transcend personal experience.

Historical context

The process of emigration and being an émigrée refers to leaving one’s own country and settling in another, either by choice or due to socio-political circumstances like war, poverty, or persecution. Written in 1993, the poem does not specify a particular country but speaks to the experiences of people forced to flee their homelands due to war, political oppression, or conflict. The late 20th century saw significant global displacement, following the fall of the Soviet Union, the Gulf War, and ongoing struggles in the Middle East and Eastern Europe leading to waves of refugees seeking safety.

Literary context

This is a contemporary poem that reflects 20th/21st century notions of migration, displacement, and personal resilience, blending the personal with the political.

Summary

This poem is written in the first person from the perspective of someone who has fled their home country and is attempting to forge a new life in a city abroad despite still feeling an inextricable link to their birthplace. It explores the psychological impact of leaving one’s home as a child when one’s impression of the world is often idealistic or naïve, hence why the speaker in the present recalls the past with such fondness. Despite their sense of exile, the speaker’s sunny memories endure as a form of defiance and preserving a connection with their country. This highly subjective memory forged in childhood may not accurately reflect reality then or now, but it is no less powerful or meaningful to the speaker.

Key ideas

- Experiences of the powerless
- Migration and dispossession
- Memory and nostalgia
- Power of self-awareness
- Lack of control over subjective experiences
- Power of place

Annotations

SNAPREVISE

There once was a country... I left it as a child
but my memory of it is sunlight-clear
for it seems I never saw it in that November
which, I am told, comes to the mildest city.
The worst news I receive of it cannot break
my original view, the bright, filled paperweight.
It may be at war, it may be sick with tyrants,
but I am branded by an impression of sunlight.

The white streets of that city, the graceful slopes
glow even clearer as time rolls its tanks
and the frontiers rise between us, close like waves.
That child's vocabulary I carried here
like a hollow doll, opens and spills a grammar.
Soon I shall have every coloured molecule of it.
It may by now be a lie, banned by the state
but I can't get it off my tongue. It tastes of sunlight.

I have no passport, there's no way back at all
but my city comes to me in its own white plane.
It lies down in front of me, docile as paper;
I comb its hair and love its shining eyes.
My city takes me dancing through the city
of walls. They accuse me of absence, they circle me.
They accuse me of being dark in their free city.
My city hides behind me. They mutter death,
and my shadow falls as evidence of sunlight.

Past tense and heavy tone of nostalgia, almost beginning like a fairy tale, immediately establishing a sense of longing for what once was; implies that either the country no longer exists, or that the version they remember from childhood no longer exists → contributes to the universality of the poem

Passive voice ("I am told") hints at external narratives conflicting with the speaker's own perception, invoking ideas of nostalgia or rose-coloured glasses

Enjambment mimics the fluidity of memory

Personification of the country as "sick with tyrants" as though it is afflicted by pain and suffering, eliciting our compassion

"White" suggests purity and peace, but may also hint at erasure or distortion of reality, but the "graceful slopes" indicate the city remains idyllic and peaceful in the speaker's mind

Enduring power of positive memories cannot be repressed by authoritarianism; synaesthesia of tasting sunlight heightens the sensory power of the memories

Both literal and metaphorical: the speaker doesn't have documents to physically return, but also cannot emotionally return to the past as they remember it

The shadow of the present proves the existence of sunlight from the past, suggesting memory persists and protects the speaker

Motif of sunlight, connoting warmth, positivity, and life force, here used to convey the intensity and clarity of the speaker's memory; motif recurs at the end of each stanza, implying a lingering power of this memory

Implies the speaker had a selective memory and did not see the hardships of "November" – perhaps a literal reference to a month when a violent event happened, or a metaphorical reference to a time of impending winter darkness and gloom

Symbolism of "paperweight" represents a frozen, unchangeable memory representing the speaker's idealised version of their homeland; despite war and tyranny, their original vision remains intact, showing emotional resistance to reality

Suggests an inescapable, ineluctable, permanent mark

Time is depicted as an oppressive force like a tank, destroying the past

"Us" further personifies the country from which the speaker is separated by "frontiers" or political and physical barriers

Lamenting that they only have a child's level of language and understanding of their home country, with the "hollow doll" being a symbol for the feeling of emptiness stemming from disconnection

Personification of the city, though this morphs from paper to a face to a dancing body, suggestive of the incorporeal/abstract version of the past that the speaker reconstructs (like trying to remember an elusive dream)

Darker tone and semantic field that suggests paranoia or outsider status – a contrast between "my city" and "they" who threaten the speaker

Theme key

- = nostalgia
- = war
- = significance of place
- = disconnection

‘Exposure’ by Wilfred Owen

SNAPREVISE

Key information

- **Poet:** Wilfred Owen (1893–1918)
- **Year:** 1920
- **Form:** Hexameter with slant rhymes
- **Key techniques:** Imagery, personification, repetition

About the poet

Wilfred Owen was one of the most influential war poets of the 20th century, known for his raw and evocative portrayal of the World War I battlefields. He developed an early love for poetry, drawing particular inspiration from John Keats and Romanticism, but his experiences as a soldier drastically changed his perspective, leading him to reject the idealistic portrayal of war in favour of stark realism. Owen enlisted as a soldier in 1915 and was later diagnosed with shell shock, which led to his hospitalisation at Craiglockhart War Hospital. There, he met Siegfried Sassoon, a fellow soldier and poet, who greatly influenced his work. Arguably his most famous poem, ‘Dulce et Decorum Est,’ explicitly critiques the notion of it being ‘sweet and fitting’ to die for one’s country.

Historical context

Wilfred Owen was a British soldier in WWI who was killed at aged 25 in 1918 a week before the war ended. His war poetry was published posthumously in 1920 and captured the gruesome realities of trench warfare as well as the psychologically devastating effects of the war on soldiers while critiquing the glorification of war.

Literary context

Owen’s poetry was influenced by classic Romantic poets like William Wordsworth and John Keats. He is considered one of the foremost War Poets of WWI alongside his friend and mentor Siegried Sassoon.

Summary

Unlike many war poems that focus on direct combat, ‘Exposure’ highlights the slow, agonising toll of having to endure the elements in the trenches. The poem consists of eight stanzas, each following a repetitive structure that mirrors the monotony and despair experienced by the soldiers. Owen uses vivid and unsettling imagery to emphasise the relentless cold, characterising “winds that knive us” and “air that shudders black with snow” to convey the physical torment. The soldiers are portrayed as trapped, powerless against nature, as they wait in a state of limbo, slowly losing hope. Through this, Owen also elucidates the futility of war as the soldiers die not from enemy fire or while mounting an attack in no man’s land, but rather from hypothermia and exhaustion. The refrain “But nothing happens” reinforces the pointlessness of their suffering. Owen also uses religious imagery to suggest that the soldiers’ suffering is akin to a kind of sacrifice, but one that leads to nothing – furthering the idea of disillusionment with war. The final lines imply that death itself becomes a relief as the soldiers resign themselves to their fate and to nothingness, and yet even after they die, “nothing happens” and the war marches on around them.

Key ideas

- Futility of war
- Psychological experience of soldiers
- Innocent victims of war
- Nature and the environment
- Exploitation of the powerless

Our brains ache, in the merciless iced east winds that knive us…
Wearied we keep awake because the night is silent…
Low drooping flares confuse our memory of the salient…
Worried by silence, sentries whisper, curious, nervous,
But nothing happens.

Watching, we hear the mad gusts tugging on the wire,
Like twitching agonies of men among its brambles.
Northward, incessantly, the flickering gunnery rumbles,
Far off, like a dull rumour of some other war.
What are we doing here?

The poignant misery of dawn begins to grow…
We only know war lasts, rain soaks, and clouds sag stormy.
Dawn massing in the east her melancholy army
Attacks once more in ranks on shivering ranks of grey,
But nothing happens.

Sudden successive flights of bullets streak the silence.
Less deadly than the air that shudders black with snow,
With sidelong flowing flakes that flock, pause, and renew,
We watch them wandering up and down the wind's nonchalance,
But nothing happens.

Pale flakes with fingering stealth come feeling for our faces—
We cringe in holes, back on forgotten dreams, and stare, snow-dazed,
Deep into grassier ditches. So we drowse, sun-dozed,
Littered with blossoms trickling where the blackbird fusses.
—Is it that we are dying?

Slowly our ghosts drag home: glimpsing the sunk fires, glozed
With crusted dark-red jewels; crickets jingle there;
For hours the innocent mice rejoice: the house is theirs;
Shutters and doors, all closed: on us the doors are closed,—
We turn back to our dying.

Since we believe not otherwise can kind fires burn;
Nor ever suns smile true on child, or field, or fruit.
For God's invincible spring our love is made afraid;
Therefore, not loath, we lie out here; therefore were born,
For love of God seems dying.

Tonight, this frost will fasten on this mud and us,
Shrivelling many hands, and puckering foreheads crisp.
The burying-party, picks and shovels in shaking grasp,
Pause over half-known faces. All their eyes are ice,
But nothing happens.

Contrast between "wearied" exhaustion and the need to be vigilant and "keep awake" suggests forced alertness and desperation

Visceral imagery that immediately establishes suffering at the hands of "merciless" nature, personified as someone stabbing them with knives

"Confuse" connotes disorientation about what is "salient" or important, alluding to a loss of purpose or understanding in war

Sibilant sounds create an oppressive hush as a blanket of cold descends on the soldiers

Slant rhyme evokes an eerie, liminal state between life and death

Symbolises the fading consciousness of the soldiers

Wind is further personified as mad; soldiers can only watch, unable to combat forces of nature

Nature reclaims territory in the soldiers' absence; they no longer belong to the world of the living

Refrain expresses the futility of war as a lack of action or resolution creates a sense of monotonous, ever-lasting suffering

Emphasises the unending, mechanical nature of war

Connotes vulnerability and resignation as the soldiers are too depleted to confront death head-on

The war feels distant from their physical reality; WWI is 'another war' separate from their fight against nature

The belief that warmth and comfort are closed to them reinforces their alienation from life

Dawn is usually a symbol of hope but is subverted or corrupted to bring misery like a hostile opposing army; all of nature is merciless, not just the harsh wind and rain

Simile equates the movement of barbed wire to the suffering of the wounded

Crisis of faith; pure emotions like love are corrupted by fear which makes them question God's benevolence (alludes to the 'problem of evil' and why God permits suffering)

Mimics chaos and unpredictability of war

Inescapable grip of death

Rhetorical question encapsulates the soldiers' existential crisis as well as literally questioning the strategic purpose for them being there just to die of exposure

Physical struggle of burial represents the toll of war on the living

Dead are reduced to anonymity

Repetition of "ranks" mirrors military formation, as though nature is coordinating an attack like a battalion

Disorienting imagery of air (which is usually invisible) shuddering, and snow (which is usually white) making the air black and thus unnatural

Graphic imagery of cold-induced death rendering the human body grotesque and unnatural

Implies the soldiers died for nothing, reinforcing the meaninglessness of death and the hollowness of justifications for war

Wind is indifferent to human suffering, reflecting the soldiers' insignificance

Bullets are less deadly than the cold, reminding us that nature is a formidable adversary

Bleak certainties conveyed in simple 'noun+verbs' sentence structures ("rain soaks") to reinforce the absolute rules and relentlessness of suffering

Theme key

- = war
- = death and suffering
- = nature
- = futility

'Kamikaze' by Beatrice Garland

Key information

- **Poet:** Beatrice Garland (1938–)
- **Year:** 2013
- **Form:** Blank verse
- **Key techniques:** Symbolism, natural imagery, enjambment

About the poet

Beatrice Garland is a British poet who has balanced a successful career as both a writer and a psychologist. Having trained as a researcher in the field of psychology and working in the NHS, Garland has studied human behaviour extensively which may have influenced her poetry's deep emotional insight. Her writing also often reflects an interest in history and culture, particularly in how individual lives are shaped by broader societal forces and major events like wars.

Historical context

Kamikaze pilots were Japanese aviators during World War II who carried out suicide missions by deliberately crashing their planes into enemy targets, primarily Allied naval vessels. Rooted in the Bushido code of honour and loyalty, these missions were seen as a last-ditch effort to defend Japan, emphasising sacrifice for the greater good, but at immense personal cost.

Literary context

This is a contemporary war poem that looks back on the experience of a soldier from a previous generation, thus aligning with modern poetry's focus on personal narratives and the power of our emotional landscapes and memories.

Summary

'Kamikaze' explores duty, honour, and the personal cost of war, told from the perspective of a woman recalling her father, a Japanese kamikaze pilot, setting out on a suicide mission but turning back after being moved by the beauty of the ocean and memories of his childhood. The pilot departs at sunrise with a clear sense of duty and adherence to tradition, but as he flies, he sees the sea and fishing boats below, triggering memories of his youth and family. This moment of reflection leads him to abandon his mission and return home. However, he finds his family and community reject him, treating him as if he no longer exists out of shame for him neglecting his duty. His wife never speaks to him again, and even his children eventually follow suit. The poem ends with a poignant question: "Which had been the better way to die?" suggesting that while he avoided physical death, he faced social and emotional erasure.

Key ideas

- Psychological experience of soldiers
- Internalisation of war
- Dehumanising impact of war
- Memory and legacy
- Power of storytelling
- Lack of control over fate

Her father embarked at sunrise
with a flask of water, a samurai sword
in the cockpit, a shaven head
full of powerful incantations
and enough fuel for a one-way
journey into history

but half way there, she thought,
recounting it later to her children,
he must have looked far down
at the little fishing boats
strung out like bunting
on a green-blue translucent sea

and beneath them, arcing in swathes
like a huge flag waved first one way
then the other in a figure of eight,
the dark shoals of fishes
flashing silver as their bellies
swivelled towards the sun

and remembered how he
and his brothers waiting on the shore
built cairns of pearl-grey pebbles
to see whose withstood longest
the turbulent inrush of breakers
bringing their father's boat safe

– yes, grandfather's boat – safe
to the shore, salt-sodden, awash
with cloud-marked mackerel,
black crabs, feathery prawns,
the loose silver of whitebait and once
a tuna, the dark prince, muscular, dangerous.

And though he came back
my mother never spoke again
in his presence, nor did she meet his eyes
and the neighbours too, they treated him
as though he no longer existed,
only we children still chattered and laughed

till gradually we too learned
to be silent, to live as though
he had never returned, that this
was no longer the father we loved.
And sometimes, she said, he must have wondered
which had been the better way to die.

Embodiment of the warrior tradition, honour, and sense of duty associated with the kamikaze's role; the ideological conditioning or propaganda reinforces the spiritual, ritualistic aspect of the mission

Connotations of a grand journey, with sunrise symbolising a new beginning, ironically challenging the nature of a kamikaze's mission

Effects of nature ravaging the vessel, conveying an abundance of life experiences → the grandfather embarked on fruitful and vibrant journeys and always returned, whereas the pilot is about to abandon his family forever

Highlights the power of legacy as pilots were expected to be martyrs, forsaking their individuality or having enough fuel to return home

Turning point of the poem where the speaker reveals her father abandoned his mission

Suggests deep shame and rejection; condemnation reflects social power

Frames the poem as an act of intergenerational storytelling, reinforcing themes of memory, legacy, and the impact of war across time

Italics represent first-person dialogue from the speaker to her children; notably the final lines of the poem are back to third-person, indicative of emotional distancing

High modal language even though the speaker is only guessing what her father saw and felt

Harrowing consequences of his decision to live, yet people do not treat him like one of the living

Contrasts the magnitude of war with the simplicity of civilian life, countering the "powerful incantations" of propaganda through peaceful, natural imagery

Denotes an irreconcilable, irrevocable divide between the memory of a loved one and their present self scarred by war or seen as flawed because of choices they made

Movement suggests harmony and continuity that is unaffected by human conflict, perhaps also swaying the pilot to set aside his wartime obligations

Speculative tone invites empathy for the pilot's torment

Contends that survival brought greater suffering than death, underscoring the severe psychological pain that soldiers endure

Fleeting, shimmering movement of the fish representing transient moments of beauty and tranquility in life

Almost all lines and stanzas in this poem are enjambed, emulating the flow of memory and stream of consciousness as the speaker's recollections rush like a flood and threaten to overwhelm us

Contrasting the grandfather's return with the pilot's doomed mission

Enjambment separates the pilot at the end of the line, but offers hope and connection to the past through the memory of his brothers in the next line

Traditionally used to mark a path to guide travellers, symbolising memory and legacy, further subverting the "one-way" singular focus of a kamikaze

Theme key

- Red = sense of duty
- Pink = interpersonal conflict
- Green = nature
- Blue = memory

‘London’ by William Blake

Key information

- **Poet:** William Blake (1757–1827)
- **Year:** 1794
- **Form:** Four quatrains, ABAB rhyme scheme
- **Key techniques:** Imagery, metaphor, repetition

About the poet

William Blake was an English poet and key figure in the Romantic movement. Born in London, he showed an early talent for drawing and was apprenticed to an engraver, which shaped his distinctive artistic style. Although he was not widely recognised during his lifetime, Blake’s work blended poetry, visual art, and mysticism in ways that later generations came to appreciate. Blake’s writing was deeply influenced by his radical political views and opposition to oppression. Blake was also known for his belief in spiritual visions, which he claimed to have seen since childhood. His art and poetry often depicted biblical themes and fantastical imagery, blending the mystical with the real.

Historical context

Published during the Industrial Revolution, a time of rapid urbanisation, economic inequality, and harsh working conditions that gave way to economic booms but also disillusionment with the new status quo. Blake also sympathsed with the French Revolution of 1789 and the ideals of liberty, equality, and fraternity.

Literary context

The poem is part of Blake’s *Songs of Experience*, a collection that contrasts with *Songs of Innocence* to explore the darker aspects of society. Blake was a Romantic poet, emphasising emotion, individual suffering, and a critique of political and religious institutions.

Summary

‘London’ presents a bleak portrait of England’s capital city, highlighting elements of suffering, oppression, and corruption. The speaker describes walking through the city while observing widespread misery and hardship. The repetition of “charter’d” emphasises the control and regulation of both people and places, including the River Thames, suggesting a lack of freedom, whilst citizens wear “marks of weakness, marks of woe” as their environment takes a physical and emotional toll on them. A key idea in the poem is the concept of “mind-forg’d manacles,” symbolising the mental and societal constraints that prevent people from escaping their suffering. Blake criticises institutions such as the Church, the monarchy, and the government, using vivid imagery like “black’ning Church” and “blood down Palace walls” to underscore their complicity in human suffering. The poem also explores the cycle of poverty and moral decay, with the final stanza depicting a young prostitute whose “curse” affects newborns and marriage, symbolising the corruption of innocence. By portraying London as a place of despair and institutional oppression, Blake delivers a powerful critique of the society of his time, with the city of London serving as a metonym for a broader erosion of values.

Key ideas

- Institutional power
- Perpetuating powerlessness and inequality
- Suffering as a consequence of conflict
- Destruction and exploitation
- The powerful vs. powerless

SNAPREVISE

I wander thro' each charter'd street,
Near where the charter'd Thames does flow.
And mark in every face I meet
Marks of weakness, marks of woe.

In every cry of every Man,
In every Infants cry of fear,
In every voice: in every ban,
The mind-forg'd manacles I hear

How the Chimney-sweepers cry
Every blackning Church appalls,
And the hapless Soldiers sigh
Runs in blood down Palace walls

But most thro' midnight streets I hear
How the youthful Harlots curse
Blasts the new-born Infants tear
And blights with plagues the Marriage hearse

"Wander" connotes aimlessness, implying the speaker is an observer rather than an active participant, reinforcing a sense of helplessness

Juxtaposition of "wander" (freedom) with "charter'd" (control) emphasises the tension between individual liberty and state authority

Repetition of "charter'd" (meaning legally mapped or controlled) highlights the excessive regulation of space, reflecting governmental and economic oppression.

Personification of the Thames as "charter'd" is striking because rivers are natural and should be free-flowing; Blake critiques the commercialisation of nature itself

Universal suffering is emphasised by repetition of "every," suggesting no one is exempt from the oppression of the city

Repetition of "marks" reinforces the permanence of suffering — these are not passing emotions but ingrained conditions — "weakness" suggests physical and emotional exhaustion, while "woe" conveys deep sorrow, implying systemic suffering rather than isolated hardship; the alliteration of "w" sounds gives a whispering, mournful tone, reinforcing the tone of despair

The noun "cry" conveys pain and helplessness, implying that oppression is so severe that it manifests audibly; the inclusion of infants means even the most innocent are subject to oppression, suggesting a vicious cycle of inherited misery

A powerful metaphor: "mind-forg'd manacles" suggests that the most insidious form of oppression is internalised, and the alliteration of "m" gives a heavy, chained effect, mirroring the idea of restraint.

Chimney sweepers were often exploited child labourers, symbolising both the loss of innocence and society's indifference to suffering

"Blackning" suggests literal soot from industrial pollution but also metaphorical corruption, implying that the Church, meant to offer hope, is tainted

Irony in the fact that the Church should be appalled/horrified by suffering, but instead is causing it as Blake contends that their religious hypocrisy enables them to turn a blind eye to the people they are meant to protect

The phrase could be an allusion to Rousseau, a key figure in the French Revolution and Enlightenment who wrote that people are born free but are mentally shackled by societal structures. Blake suggests that oppression is not just physical but psychological, as people accept and reinforce their own subjugation.

"Sigh" conveys exhaustion and disillusionment, highlighting the futility of war

Striking image linking war to the monarchy, suggesting that the ruling class is responsible for the bloodshed of soldiers, and that unchecked oppression may lead to violent rebellion when the powerful are complicit

"Blasts" is a violent verb, implying that the prostitute's suffering negatively impacts the next generation. The baby's first experience of life is one of sorrow, reinforcing the cyclical nature of oppression. The final imagery critiques both societal hypocrisy and the destruction of traditional institutions by poverty and oppression.

The oxymoron "youthful Harlot" juxtaposes innocence with corruption, emphasising how society forces young women into prostitution

The oxymoron "Marriage hearse" combines love and death, implying that marriage — a supposed institution of hope — is tainted by "blight" connoting disease and decay, possibly alluding to the spread of venereal disease that was thought to be linked to moral corruption

Theme key

- Red = suffering
- Pink = institutions and oppression
- Green = nature
- Blue = corruption

'My Last Duchess' by Robert Browning

Key information

- **Poet:** Robert Browning (1812–1889)
- **Year:** 1842
- **Form:** Dramatic monologue in iambic pentameter
- **Key techniques:** Foreshadowing, repetition, irony

About the poet

Robert Browning was a renowned English poet and playwright, best known for his mastery of the dramatic monologue as seen in this poem. He was largely self-educated, developing an early love for literature and languages. In 1846, Browning married fellow poet Elizabeth Barrett and moved to Italy. This period was one of great literary productivity for Browning, but it was only after Elizabeth's death in 1861 that his reputation truly flourished. He died in 1889 and was buried in Westminster Abbey's Poets' Corner as one of the most influential poets of the 19th century.

Historical context

This poem was written during the Victorian era, a period marked by strict social hierarchies and patriarchal control over women. It is set in Renaissance Italy and is loosely based on the life of Alfonso II, Duke of Ferrara, whose young wife, Lucrezia de' Medici, died under suspicious circumstances. The themes of power, control, and gender roles reflect both the historical setting of the poem and Victorian anxieties about marriage and female autonomy.

Literary context

The poem is a dramatic monologue, a form that Browning popularised, allowing readers to explore the speaker's psychology through his speech. It follows the traditions of Gothic and Romantic literature, emphasising themes of power, obsession, and the darker aspects of human nature through its critique of aristocratic vanity and the commodification of women in marriage.

Summary

'My Last Duchess' is a dramatic monologue in which a powerful Duke speaks to a visitor about a portrait of his late wife. As the Duke shows the painting, he describes the Duchess as beautiful and easily pleased, but his tone quickly reveals his jealousy and controlling nature. He resents the way she smiled at others and took delight in simple pleasures, believing that her behaviour did not properly honour his status. The Duke hints that he had her killed, implying he "gave commands; / Then all smiles stopped together." His casual mention of this act showcases his arrogance and sense of entitlement. The monologue takes place as he negotiates a new marriage, subtly warning the listener (likely an envoy) about the kind of wife he expects. The poem explores themes of power, control, and gender roles, portraying the Duke as a manipulative and egotistical figure who views women as possessions. Through his speech, Browning exposes the dark side of aristocracy and the dangers of unchecked authority. The poem's unsettling tone and the Duke's chilling revelations make it one of Browning's most famous and psychologically complex works.

Key ideas

- Exerting power over other people
- Jealousy and possessiveness
- Gender oppression
- Powerful vs. the powerless
- Memory

Annotations

SNAPREVISE

Possessive pronoun "my" by which the Duke asserts ownership over the Duchess and asserts his ownership

Hypothetical ominously hints at her death

That's my last Duchess painted on the wall,
Looking as if she were alive. I call
That piece a wonder, now; Fra Pandolf's hands
Worked busily a day, and there she stands.
Will't please you sit and look at her? I said
"Fra Pandolf" by design, for never read
Strangers like you that pictured countenance,
The depth and passion of its earnest glance,
But to myself they turned (since none puts by
The curtain I have drawn for you, but I)
And seemed as they would ask me, if they durst,
How such a glance came there; so, not the first
Are you to turn and ask thus. Sir, 'twas not
Her husband's presence only, called that spot
Of joy into the Duchess' cheek; perhaps
Fra Pandolf chanced to say, "Her mantle laps
Over my lady's wrist too much," or "Paint
Must never hope to reproduce the faint
Half-flush that dies along her throat." Such stuff
Was courtesy, she thought, and cause enough
For calling up that spot of joy. She had
A heart—how shall I say?—too soon made glad,
Too easily impressed; she liked whate'er
She looked on, and her looks went everywhere.
Sir, 'twas all one! My favour at her breast,
The dropping of the daylight in the West,
The bough of cherries some officious fool
Broke in the orchard for her, the white mule
She rode with round the terrace—all and each
Would draw from her alike the approving speech,

He sees the art as a wonder, not her

A fictional painter whose name underscores the Duke's obsession with prestige and status, especially as the name is repeated again in lines 6 and 16

The Duke feigns politeness with a rhetorical question and asserts dominance over the listener

Parenthetical remark reinforces the Duke's absolute control; he decides who views the Duchess' "depth and passion," reinforcing his possessiveness

Meaning "if they dare" — the Duke's past listeners dared not question him, hinting at his intimidating presence

He trivializes the Duchess's natural responses, implying she was too naïve or flirtatious but he sees this as a betrayal

"Half-flush" imagery suggests innocence but is immediately followed by "dies along her throat" — a threatening shift that betrays the Duke's fear of evidence of infidelity

Implies she was fickle and disloyal, impressed by anyone and everyone, thus the Duke tries to justify his mistreatment of her

Listing/asyndeton to imply the Duchess appreciates simple joys, which the Duke resents as she does not prioritise him

He belittles those who please the Duchess, further reiterating his jealousy

Tone of aristocratic pride; the Duke values the lineage of his "nine-hundred years-old name" over love, showing his elitism and implying she should be more grateful for his marriage offer than any "trifling" gift

Or blush, at least. She thanked men—good! but thanked
Somehow—I know not how—as if she ranked
My gift of a nine-hundred-years-old name
With anybody's gift. Who'd stoop to blame
This sort of trifling? Even had you skill
In speech—which I have not—to make your will
Quite clear to such an one, and say, "Just this
Or that in you disgusts me; here you miss,
Or there exceed the mark"—and if she let
Herself be lessoned so, nor plainly set
Her wits to yours, forsooth, and made excuse—
E'en then would be some stooping; and I choose
Never to stoop. Oh, sir, she smiled, no doubt,
Whene'er I passed her; but who passed without
Much the same smile? This grew; I gave commands;
Then all smiles stopped together. There she stands
As if alive. Will't please you rise? We'll meet
The company below, then. I repeat,
The Count your master's known munificence
Is ample warrant that no just pretense
Of mine for dowry will be disallowed;
Though his fair daughter's self, as I avowed
At starting, is my object. Nay, we'll go
Together down, sir. Notice Neptune, though,
Taming a sea-horse, thought a rarity,
Which Claus of Innsbruck cast in bronze for me!

Hypocrisy and faux-humility; pretending to lack rhetorical skill and hide his power when in fact his monologue is carefully crafted

His true feelings are hidden in this hypothetical dialogue

He resents her for having free will and speaking back using her wits instead of being "lessoned"/deferential

He refuses to "stoop" to her level or debase himself by conversing with her as an equal suggesting rigid pride

A chilling, menacingly vague euphemism, implying he ordered her death

Conveys sinister finality as her joy is permanently silenced and only immortalised in his painting of her

Abrupt shift to discuss his next marriage, betraying a lack of remorse and materialistic concerns over the "dowry" transaction rather than emotional connection

Allusion to the Roman God Neptune "taming" an animal represents the Duke's desire to dominate and control, and his delusions of grandeur

Poem concludes with the Duke moving on to brag about the next piece of artwork in his collection, exhibiting cold detachment from the memory of his first wife and treating it as just another object "for me!" to boast of

Theme key

- = ownership
- = death and foreshadowing
- = objectification
- = superiority

'Ozymandias' by Percy Bysshe Shelley

SNAPREVISE

Key information

- **Poet:** Percy Bysshe Shelley (1792–1822)
- **Year:** 1818
- **Form:** Sonnet in iambic pentameter (three quatrains with a rhyming couplet at the end)
- **Key techniques:** Caesura, situational irony, vivid imagery, allegory

About the poet

Percy Bysshe Shelley was a poet known for his radical politics, lyrical mastery, philosophical depth, and reverence for nature. Born into an aristocratic family in Sussex, he attended Oxford University but was expelled in 1811 for publishing an essay called 'The Necessity of Atheism.' His unorthodox beliefs, including opposition to monarchy, organised religion, and social inequality, shaped both his personal life and literary works. In 1816 he married Mary Wollstonecraft Godwin who would go on to write *Frankenstein* as Mary Shelley, with contributions from Percy Shelley. Exiled from Britain in 1818 due to his radicalism, Shelley spent much of his life in Italy, where he befriended fellow poets Lord Byron and John Keats. His untimely death at 29 when he drowned in a boating accident cemented his status as a tragic literary figure. Though largely unappreciated during his lifetime, Shelley is now recognised as one of the greatest poets of the English Romantic movement.

Summary

'Ozymandias' exposes the impermanence of human power. The poem is framed as a traveller regaling the speaker of their encounter with a ruined statue in the desert. The shattered remains depict a once-mighty ruler named Ozymandias, with a "sneer of cold command," suggesting his arrogance and authoritarian rule. The pedestal bears an inscription boasting of his greatness: "Look on my Works, ye Mighty, and despair!" However, there is a palpable and tragic irony – his empire has vanished, and nothing remains but "boundless and bare" sands stretching into the distance. Through this contrast between past glory and present decay, Shelley critiques the hubris of tyrants and the fleeting nature of political power. The poem also highlights the enduring power of art – the sculptor's depiction of Ozymandias' expression outlives his empire. The use of vivid imagery, irony, and a fragmented narrative structure reinforces the theme that all human achievements and powers, no matter how grand, are ultimately consumed by time.

Historical context

This poem was inspired by the recent discovery of a fragmentary statue of Pharaoh Ramesses II, also known as Ozymandias, which was being transported to the British Museum. The poem reflects the fascination of the Romantic era with ancient civilizations, particularly Egypt, which was being explored by European archaeologists. Shelley uses the poem to critique the fleeting nature of power, echoing contemporary political upheavals, such as the fall of Napoleon.

Key ideas

- Transience of power
- Hubris of tyrants
- Power of the natural world
- Man vs. nature

Literary context

'Ozymandias' is a sonnet that fits within the Romantic tradition, emphasising nature's power over human achievements. The poem aligns with Shelley's broader themes of political critique, the impermanence of human glory, and the limits of tyranny. It also reflects the ancient idea of memento mori – a Latin phrase meaning 'remember you will die' that serves as a reminder that life, power, and control are all temporary.

Framing device for the poem – we hear this information second-hand, aligning us with the mysterious speaker who learns about the existence of the statue as we do

The possible unreliable narration from the unknown "traveller" from an unspecified place adds a layer of ambiguity, emphasising Ozymandias' fading legacy

Diction of "an antique land" evokes an ancient, almost mythical past, foreshadowing the passage of time

Contrast between size and incompleteness in "vast and trunkless" highlights decay and is almost oxymoronic – the features of the statue are "vast" = expansive and immeasurable, and yet "trunkless" = detached from the body/trunk and clearly fragmented

Caesura after "Who said" slows the pace, making the reader pause yet creating the sense of a story starting mid-way through this line

Symbolism of legs suggests strength, but the lack of torso signals the fragility of human power

Ellipsis creates a dramatic pause as well as a lack of action taken by the legs that stand in the desert... but don't do anything

Desert symbolises emptiness and a harsh environment capable of erasing human ambition and reinforcing nature's supremacy

I met a traveller from an antique land,
Who said—"Two vast and trunkless legs of stone
Stand in the desert... Near them, on the sand,
Half sunk a shattered visage lies, whose frown,
And wrinkled lip, and sneer of cold command,
Tell that its sculptor well those passions read
Which yet survive, stamped on these lifeless things,
The hand that mocked them, and the heart that fed;
And on the pedestal, these words appear:
My name is Ozymandias, King of Kings;
Look on my Works, ye Mighty, and despair!
Nothing beside remains. Round the decay
Of that colossal Wreck, boundless and bare
The lone and level sands stretch far away."

"Half sunk" and "shattered" characterises the face as broken and buried, representing the erosion of Ozymandias' power

The fact that the face lies on the sand suggests the statue has been defeated, as if abandoned by history

"Visage" is a grandiose word befitting a ruler, yet there is irony as his empire is gone, subverting the seeming permanence of his power

Tyrant's expression characterised through alliteration "cold command" and words connoting arrogance like "sneer" to emphasise his hubris, all of which is undermined and rendered impotent by his ruined state

Suggests the sculptor's skill has immortalised the ruler's cruelty/tyranny rather than his glory, showing how art preserves truth

"Stamped" implies forceful imposition, as if Ozymandias's cruelty was imprinted on history, yet this vision of cruelty outlives him through art, contrasting vitality with ruin

Synecdoche of "hand" and "heart" reduces the king to body parts, dehumanising him; the hand (artist's craft) outlasts the heart (ruler's ego/ambition), reinforcing art's permanence and power over fickle human desires

Words on the pedestal further immortalised, though are rife with dramatic irony since Ozymandias' declaration is no longer relevant to modern civilisation

Biblical allusion to "King of Kings" (an epithet used for Jesus Christ) evokes religious grandeur and hubris, perhaps suggesting Ozymandias' blasphemous conviction was somewhat responsible for his fall, even though this tone of absolute, high modality and confidence in his own supremacy is undermined by his erasure from history and current state of disrepair

Imperative command asserts dominance even long after his reign; "my Works" is intended to impress or intimidate, but now unintentionally draws attention to the emptiness of his legacy as there are no works to look upon – "nothing beside remains" – thus people despair not at his power, but at its complete disappearance

Ambiguity: could be 'there is nothing except for these remains,' or 'nothing is next to this fallen statue' – both possibilities emphasise stark, lonely desolation

Oxymoron of "colossal Wreck" pairs grandeur with destruction, reinforcing the situational irony

Sibilance in "sands stretch" mimics the whispering of the empty desert and imbues the poem with one last ironic note: Ozymandias sought eternal glory, but only the endless sands endure

Theme key

- red = hubris/pride
- pink = subjectivity
- green = impotence/fragility
- blue = passage of time

'Poppies' by Jane Weir

SNAPREVISE

Key information

- **Poet:** Jane Weir (1963–)
- **Year:** 2005
- **Form:** Free verse
- **Key techniques:** Second-person POV, sensory imagery, symbolism, caesura, motif of clothing

About the poet

Jane Weir is a British poet, novelist, and designer who often draws upon her Anglo-Italian heritage in her writing. She is particularly renowned for her poetry that gives voice to untold perspectives, particularly women's experiences of war, offering insights into both past and present conflicts and making her a significant figure in contemporary British literature.

Historical context

Poppies are a potent symbol of remembrance and hope for a peaceful future after war, originating in World War I but now taking on broader symbolism for all armed forces. This poem was written at a time when British soldiers were fighting in conflicts in Afghanistan and Iraq, reflecting the personal grief and loss experienced by families, particularly mothers, drawing on the tradition of war poetry while focusing on the impact on those left behind.

Literary context

In 2005, the poet Carol Ann Duffy commissioned various poets including Weir to write poems to honour the sacrifices made by British soldiers in the Middle East. These poems were published in a collection called *Exit Wounds*.

Summary

'Poppies' is written from the perspective of a mother before and after her son's departure for military service, blending past and present through a stream-of-consciousness narrative. The mother recalls pinning a poppy to her son's blazer, a symbol of both remembrance and impending loss. Her small, intimate gestures such as smoothing his collar and resisting the urge to touch his hair highlight her deep love and reluctance to let go. As he leaves, she describes the outside world as "overflowing like a treasure chest," capturing his excitement in contrast to her silent grief. After his departure, she enters his empty bedroom, metaphorically "releasing a songbird from its cage," suggesting both freedom and loss. The imagery of "a single dove" and her walk to the war memorial reinforce themes of remembrance, longing, and absence. The ambiguous ending leaves the reader questioning whether her son has died or simply never returned. Thus, the poem ultimately presents the quiet, personal cost of war, focusing on the pain experienced by those left behind rather than those on the battlefield itself.

Key ideas

- Power of memories
- Family connection and legacy
- Innocent victims of war
- Personal and emotional loss
- Power of sacrifice

Three days before Armistice Sunday
and poppies had already been placed
on individual war graves. Before you left,
I pinned one onto your lapel, crimped petals,
spasms of paper red, disrupting a blockade
of yellow bias binding around your blazer.

Sellotape bandaged around my hand,
I rounded up as many white cat hairs
as I could, smoothed down your shirt's
upturned collar, steeled the softening
of my face. I wanted to graze my nose
across the tip of your nose, play at
being Eskimos like we did when
you were little. I resisted the impulse
to run my fingers through the gelled
blackthorns of your hair. All my words
flattened, rolled, turned into felt,

slowly melting. I was brave, as I walked
with you, to the front door, threw
it open, the world overflowing
like a treasure chest. A split second
and you were away, intoxicated.
After you'd gone I went into your bedroom,
released a song bird from its cage.
Later a single dove flew from the pear tree,
and this is where it has led me,
skirting the church yard walls, my stomach busy
making tucks, darts, pleats, hat-less, without
a winter coat or reinforcements of scarf, gloves.

On reaching the top of the hill I traced
the inscriptions on the war memorial,
leaned against it like a wishbone.
The dove pulled freely against the sky,
an ornamental stitch. I listened, hoping to hear
your playground voice catching on the wind.

Passive construction "had already been placed" distances the speaker from the act, hinting at emotional detachment

Reference to Armistice Sunday immediately situates the poem in the context of WWI, evoking collective remembrance

The pinned poppy is a symbolic parting gift and a memory of a caring gesture, foreshadowing death and sacrifice

Caesura and temporal shift pulls us back to the past, like the poppies have triggered a flashback

Asyndeton of sensory details conveys a sense of vivid memory; this is implied to be the last time the speaker saw her son, thereby heightening the significance of every small detail

Evocative of bloodshed and pain

Lack of temporal specificity implies time no longer matters now that her son is gone

Transforms a domestic action of cleaning clothes into an act of care and quiet suffering, the verb "bandaged" connoting wounds and first aid

Familiar gestures of tidying are emblematic of the speaker's maternal instinct used to distract herself and suppress deeper emotions and fears – she must be "steeled" and not "soft" in front of her child, even in sending him to war

"Blackthorns" suggests both the sharpness of adulthood and a crown of thorns, reinforcing sacrificial imagery

Tender, child-like imagery juxtaposes past intimacy with present formality and impending separation, making the moment more poignant. The nostalgic 'Eskimo kiss' is a ritual of affection she must now deny herself, and tragically will never experience again

Felt is soft yet dense, symbolising muffled grief – emotion is subdued but ever-present. This could also be evocative of children's toys or clothes which are often made of felt, suggesting her emotions have been reduced to something child-like and primitive

"Slowly melting" suggests emotional surrender, but in a restrained manner with the enjambment from stanza 2 to 3 representing the bleeding of memories across time

Excessive caesural pauses mirror the mother's hesitation and grief, as though she is choking up with emotion

Optimistic simile connoting rewards, contrasting with the mother's internal emptiness and hollow promises of WWI glory

Contrast "Before you left" from line 3 with "After you'd gone" as two distinct chapters in the speaker's mind, defining her life by the presence and absence of her son

Song bird = the mother's suppressed grief finally unleashed now that she doesn't have to put on a brave face

Likens her internal turmoil to fabric being shaped by forces beyond its control – a contrast to the son's smoothed uniform from earlier

Vulnerability and exposure, paralleling WWI soldiers often ill-prepared for battle

Redolent of Remembrance Day commemorations

Dove symbolises peace, the soul, and death, hinting at the son's fate. Here, the dove is contrasted with ornamental stitch, linking the imagery of nature and textiles; the stitch may symbolise both permanence and fragility – grief is woven into her existence

Wishbone simile suggests fragility, fate, and the unfulfilled hope of reunion

The poem ends with auditory longing: her son's voice is absent, yet she listens for it, caught between memory and reality

Theme key

- = war and death
- = emotional loss
- = family
- = time and memory

‘The Prelude’ by William Wordsworth

Key information

- **Poet:** William Wordsworth (1770–1850)
- **Year:** 1798
- **Form:** Epic poem, iambic pentameter/blank verse
- **Key techniques:** Natural imagery, personification, contrast

About the poet

William Wordsworth was a key figure in the Romantic movement known for his deep reverence for nature and the sublime. He spent much of his childhood in the scenic Lake District, which greatly influenced his poetry. After losing both parents at a young age, he was educated at Cambridge but found true inspiration during his travels in France, where he initially embraced revolutionary ideals. In 1795, he formed a close friendship with Samuel Taylor Coleridge, leading to the publication of *Lyrical Ballads* (1798), a collection that redefined English poetry by emphasising ordinary language and nature's spiritual significance. He later served as Poet Laureate from 1843 until his death in 1850. His magnum opus, *The Prelude*, was an autobiographical epic, tracing his personal and intellectual development. This work, though unpublished during his lifetime, became one of the most influential Romantic poems.

Historical context

This poem is an excerpt of a much longer (400+ line) epic poem written during a period of immense political and social change including the French Revolution and the Industrial Revolution in England. Wordsworth was influenced by the revolutionary ideas of liberty and individual experience, but as he matured, he became disillusioned with radical politics, shifting towards a more introspective exploration of personal and natural influences. His writing also expresses a longing for the unspoiled beauty of nature in contrast to the mechanisation of industrialised society.

Summary

The full poem *The Prelude* is a long autobiographical poem reflecting on the poet's development and his deep relationship with nature. This excerpt describes a childhood experience in which the speaker takes a boat without permission, initially feeling excitement and freedom as he rows across the lake. The imagery of the water, moonlight, and smooth rowing conveys a sense of harmony between the speaker and nature. However, this peacefulness is disrupted when a massive mountain peak suddenly comes into view, personified as a towering, menacing presence. The speaker feels pursued by the mountain, as if it moves with intent, instilling in him a deep fear and realization of nature's overwhelming power. This encounter changes his perception, as his youthful confidence gives way to a humbling awareness of nature's grandeur and his own insignificance. For days afterward, the experience lingers in his mind, casting a shadow over his thoughts and dreams. The poem explores themes of the sublime, where nature evokes both awe and fear, and highlights how such moments shape personal growth. Wordsworth suggests that childhood encounters with nature have a lasting impact, influencing one's understanding of the world and the self.

Key ideas

- Power of nature
- Power of personal experiences
- Power of memory
- Subjectivity and reality

Literary context

Wordsworth was heavily influenced by Milton's *Paradise Lost*, as seen in his use of blank verse and grand, introspective tone that elevates his personal experience to one of universal significance, emphasising the power of individual emotions and one's sublime connection to nature.

One summer evening (led by her) I found
A little boat tied to a willow tree
Within a rocky cove, its usual home.
Straight I unloosed her chain, and stepping in
Pushed from the shore. It was an act of stealth
And troubled pleasure, nor without the voice
Of mountain-echoes did my boat move on;
Leaving behind her still, on either side,
Small circles glittering idly in the moon,
Until they melted all into one track
Of sparkling light. But now, like one who rows,
Proud of his skill, to reach a chosen point
With an unswerving line, I fixed my view
Upon the summit of a craggy ridge,
The horizon's utmost boundary; far above
Was nothing but the stars and the grey sky.
She was an elfin pinnace; lustily
I dipped my oars into the silent lake,
And, as I rose upon the stroke, my boat
Went heaving through the water like a swan;
When, from behind that craggy steep till then
The horizon's bound, a huge peak, black and huge,
As if with voluntary power instinct,
Upreared its head. I struck and struck again,
And growing still in stature the grim shape
Towered up between me and the stars, and still,
For so it seemed, with purpose of its own
And measured motion like a living thing,
Strode after me. With trembling oars I turned,
And through the silent water stole my way
Back to the covert of the willow tree;
There in her mooring-place I left my bark, –
And through the meadows homeward went, in grave
And serious mood; but after I had seen
That spectacle, for many days, my brain
Worked with a dim and undetermined sense
Of unknown modes of being; o'er my thoughts
There hung a darkness, call it solitude
Or blank desertion. No familiar shapes
Remained, no pleasant images of trees,
Of sea or sky, no colours of green fields;
But huge and mighty forms, that do not live
Like living men, moved slowly through the mind
By day, and were a trouble to my dreams.

Peaceful and idyllic imagery complimented by gentle assonance of "little" and "willow"

Personification of nature as a woman leading the speaker like a guiding force or a partner

Connotes freedom and agency as the boat too is personified – a symbolic vessel for the poet's journey of self-discovery

Leaving the shore and the usual home is indicative of the start of a 'hero's journey'

oxymoron hints at unease or uncertainty

The "voice" of the mountain echoes, suggesting nature is actively responding to the speaker's presence

Semantic field of a shimmering, dreamlike atmosphere

Suggests focused ambition and deliberate direction, a contrast to the earlier passive guidance by nature

Emphasises vastness of nature and the comparative insignificance of human presence within it

Diction of "lustily" and "heaving" draw attention to the speaker's corporeal body and have almost sexual connotations, heightening the poem's intensity

Suggests a magical, fairy-like quality to the boat

Simile/symbol of grace and effortlessness

Represents a physical and metaphorical boundary between the known and unknown

"Mighty forms" move through his mind, suggesting lingering awe and fear long after the journey is over

Represents the overwhelming power of nature and its unfathomable impact on human consciousness

The lack of anything familiar or pleasant underscores a drastic departure from the poem's initially bucolic, care-free beginning

Repetition of "huge peak, black and huge" amplifies the mountain's imposing presence, as though it is so huge that it needs to be called huge twice!

The peak disrupts the previously peaceful, controlled experience and also seems to be personified as having its own head and threatening intentions, later growing and towering as if alive

The mountain obstructing the stars suggests a loss of guidance and connection with the entirety of nature

The mountain pursues the speaker; its unknowable "purpose of its own" makes it all the more frightening and uncanny (i.e. it's not just that the mountain is moving, but that it wants to move for some reason)

"Trembling" and "covert" emphasises fear and the return to stealth/safety, having had one's vulnerability exposed

Shift from fear to introspection; "unknown modes" suggests existential contemplation while "darkness" metaphorically hangs over his mind

Theme key

- (red) = feeling of awe
- (pink) = personal journey
- (green) = power of nature
- (blue) = mystery/the unknown

'Remains' by Simon Armitage

Key information

- **Poet:** Simon Armitage (1963–)
- **Year:** 2008
- **Form:** Free verse
- **Key techniques:** Colloquial language, graphic imagery, repetition

About the poet

Simon Armitage is a contemporary British writer and the current Poet Laureate of the United Kingdom (2019–2029). He first worked as a probation officer, having obtained an MA in social work, before becoming a full-time writer. His poetry is known for its direct, conversational tone and focus on the experiences of ordinary people. His poems often focus on war, its psychological impact, and the inner emotional landscapes of soldiers.

Historical context

This poem reflects the experience of post-traumatic stress disorder (PTSD) experienced by veterans, particularly British soldiers returning from Iraq and Afghanistan during the 2000s.

Literary context

This poem is part of a collection called *The Not Dead* which explores the psychological scars inflicted on those who survive a war. In keeping with the rich history of war poetry as a genre from earlier conflicts, most notably the work of Wilfred Owen whose WWI poems touched on the same ideas of trauma (then called 'shell shock'), Armitage's work emphasises the horrors of war by depicting its impact on the human mind. He was also influenced by poets like Ted Hughes and Philip Larkin who combine sharp observations with social commentary.

Summary

'Remains' explores the psychological trauma of a soldier haunted by his actions during war. In the poem, the soldier recounts an incident where he and his comrades shot a suspected looter. The repetition of "probably armed, possibly not" highlights the uncertainty and moral culpability the soldier feels about whether the killing was justified. As the poem progresses, it shifts from a description of the event to the long-term impact on the soldier's mental state. Even after returning home, he cannot escape his memories – "he bursts again through the doors of the bank" in his dreams. The use of enjambment and fragmented structure mirrors the soldier's disjointed thoughts, showing how war has left him psychologically broken. The final lines, "his bloody life in my bloody hands" is reminiscent of *Macbeth* and one of the most famous symbols in Shakespeare where Lady Macbeth hallucinates blood on her hands that represents guilt and inescapable trauma. The poem critiques the dehumanising nature of war, exposing how soldiers are left to deal with their guilt alone, long after the conflict has ended.

Key ideas

- Psychological trauma of war
- Guilt and moral ambiguity
- Lasting effects of war
- Loss of control over one's life

On another occasion, we got sent out
to tackle looters raiding a bank.
And one of them legs it up the road,
probably armed, possibly not.

Well myself and somebody else and somebody else
are all of the same mind,
so all three of us open fire.
Three of a kind all letting fly, and I swear

I see every round as it rips through his life –
I see broad daylight on the other side.
So we've hit this looter a dozen times
and he's there on the ground, sort of inside out,

pain itself, the image of agony.
One of my mates goes by
and tosses his guts back into his body.
Then he's carted off in the back of a lorry.

End of story, except not really.
His blood-shadow stays on the street, and out on patrol
I walk right over it week after week.
Then I'm home on leave. But I blink

and he bursts again through the doors of the bank.
Sleep, and he's probably armed, and possibly not.
Dream, and he's torn apart by a dozen rounds.
And the drink and the drugs won't flush him out –

he's here in my head when I close my eyes,
dug in behind enemy lines,
not left for dead in some distant, sun-stunned, sand-smothered land
or six-feet-under in desert sand,

but near to the knuckle, here and now,
his bloody life in my bloody hands.

Almost in media res opening as though the speaker has just finished telling us about one "occasion" and is switching to another, suggesting routine violence and desensitisation as events blur together

Passive sentence, shifting blame those who sent them?

Low modal "probably" and "possibly" emphasises doubt and hints at moral conflict over the killing, though notably the speaker leans more towards "probably armed," only allowing himself to admit "possibly not" as this possibility scares him more

"Looters" connotes criminality but also desperation

Unifies the men, but this camaraderie is warped into a sinister force making all three men shoot a possibly unarmed civilian without hesitating

Vague anonymity of "somebody else" could be seen as shielding his fellow men from blame, but also reduces the individuality of the soldiers as though they are just units acting on instinct, not people with conscience

Every round hits, so all three men are responsible, whereas typically a firing squad would have some blanks, allowing each person to feel they may not have been personally responsible

Euphemisms and colloquialisms lack emotional weight, reflecting how violence is normalised as well as minimising the carnage

Horrifying imagery, making the violence even more graphic and confronting while also positioning the reader to observe the scene from the perspective of the soldier seeing sunlight shine through the holes in a person's body

Disturbingly casual, indirect language that betrays emotional detachment while also vividly depicting the horror of the scene

Gruesome imagery, a lack of dignity in death – his guts and body now reduced to waste to be "tosse[d]" and "carted off"

"Pain itself" turns suffering into a physical presence, highlighting the horror of death and searing the imagery into the speaker's memory

"Blood-shadow" metaphor for lingering guilt; the unusual diction makes this even more haunting (not a blood stain, but a blood shadow cast by an unknown source)

"End of story" occurring halfway through the poem and at the start of the stanza clearly undermines itself, suggesting an attempt to dismiss the event ignores the soldier's deep trauma

Present tense shows how the memories are still vivid and intrusive

Enjambment across stanzas creates a fragmented sense of horror, emulating a sudden PTSD flashback

Ratcheting up fear as the speaker describes a source of terror like a hidden enemy that lives within his own head

Militaristic language describing the memory of the dead man as an enemy force that is "dug in" and can't be "flush[ed] out" using traditional tactics

Self-destructive coping mechanisms are ineffective

Redolent of Lady Macbeth's "Out, damn'd spot" soliloquy in which she is driven mad by a blood stain that will not wash out – a manifestation of her guilt at having been complicit in the murder of innocent people

Ends with unresolved trauma and a sense of inescapable guilt, implying that wartime experiences have lasting consequences

"Sun-stunned, sand-smothered" creates a hypnotic effect, emphasising the oppressive, suffocating nature of PTSD

Theme key

- = guilt
- = desensitisation
- = moral ambiguity
- = memory

Key information

- **Poet:** Seamus Heaney (1939–2013)
- **Year:** 1966
- **Form:** Blank verse
- **Key techniques:** Violent imagery, irony, metaphor

About the poet

Seamus Heaney was an Irish poet and playwright born in County Derry, Northern Ireland, to a farming family, which deeply influenced his poetry's themes of rural life and Irish identity. Heaney studied at Queen's University Belfast before becoming a teacher and later a full-time poet. His first major collection, *Death of a Naturalist* (1966), established him as poet capable of blending rich natural imagery with personal and political themes. Over the years, his work increasingly addressed the tensions in Northern Ireland, particularly during The Troubles, while still maintaining a deep connection to the Irish landscape and history. He was awarded the Nobel Prize in Literature in 1995, praised for his "works of lyrical beauty and ethical depth."

Historical context

This poem reflects the harsh natural conditions faced by island communities, particularly in Ireland. It can also be interpreted as an allegory for the political turbulence of The Troubles in Northern Ireland (1960s–1998), where violence and unrest were constant yet often invisible threats and powerful forces, much like a storm.

Literary context

The poem is part of Heaney's 1966 collection *Death of a Naturalist* which explores nature, rural life, and human vulnerability. It builds upon the tradition of pastoral poetry, yet instead of romanticising nature, Heaney presents it as an overwhelming and destructive force. The poem also reflects modernist influences, using free verse and fragmented imagery to capture the chaotic, unpredictable storm.

Summary

'Storm on the Island' explores the immense power of nature and the vulnerability of human existence. The poem describes an island community preparing for a storm, highlighting their practical resilience as they build strong houses to withstand the brutal weather. Heaney contrasts the emptiness of the landscape with the violent energy of the storm, using military metaphors to liken the storm's attack to warfare. The islanders face an invisible but overwhelming force, reinforcing the notion of fear of the unknown. The sea, initially seen as "company," turns hostile, much like a "tame cat turned savage." This transformation mirrors how familiar elements of life can suddenly become dangerous and unpredictable. The final line, "Strange, it is a huge nothing that we fear," encapsulates the poem's central paradox: the storm is both a physical reality and an abstract threat. This suggests a deeper meaning beyond its literal focus on a storm as Heaney subtly alludes to political unrest in Northern Ireland, where an unseen yet ever-present danger loomed over daily life. Thus, the poem presents both nature and human existence as forces shaped by unpredictability, resilience, and fear.

Key ideas

- Power of nature
- Human resilience
- Fear of the unknown
- Lack of control over one's life
- Feeling powerlessness

Annotations

We are prepared: we build our houses squat,
Sink walls in rock and roof them with good slate.
The wizened earth had never troubled us
With hay, so as you can see, there are no stacks
Or stooks that can be lost. Nor are there trees
Which might prove company when it blows full
Blast: you know what I mean – leaves and branches
Can raise a chorus in a gale
So that you can listen to the thing you fear
Forgetting that it pummels your house too.
But there are no trees, no natural shelter.
You might think that the sea is company,
Exploding comfortably down on the cliffs
But no: when it begins, the flung spray hits
The very windows, spits like a tame cat
Turned savage. We just sit tight while wind dives
And strafes invisibly. Space is a salvo.
We are bombarded by the empty air.
Strange, it is a huge nothing that we fear.

Collective pronoun "we" establishes a sense of community and shared experience, hinting at resilience and strength in numbers; being prepared denotes confidence, foresight, and security, though also implies there is some future peril yet to come

Indicate sturdiness and practicality in response to natural forces

Personification of the land as "wizened" meaning aged or barren suggests a harsh, infertile environment

Tone of quiet pride as it implies the earth doesn't trouble the speaker because their community is so prepared and practical in adapting to the land; in combination with "wizened" it also suggests this community has withstood the harsh environment for a long time, indicative of intergenerational strength

"Stacks / Or stooks" are agricultural terms for stored crops; the lack of supplies and land that does not yield crops suggests the people must be even more hardy and self-sufficient to endure their circumstances

Repetition of "no" and "nor" reinforces the barrenness of the location, defined by what it lacks – in fact there is nothing "that can be lost" which implies the people are even more powerful to be able to forge a life in such a hostile place with no resources

Plosive alliteration of "blows" and "blast" emphasises the power of the wind

Personification of trees that could provide "company" and comfort, but instead their absence isolates the people and forces them to confront their loneliness

"Chorus" gives nature a melodic voice whilst "gale" infers a chaotic, overwhelming force

Abstract, vague wording makes fear seem intangible yet ever-present

Conversational tone of creates intimacy and implies shared experience

Violent verb that reinforces the relentless wind

Suggests the power of nature is so awe-inspiring that you could listen to its fearsome power and completely lose sight of how it is endangering you

Again, repetition of "no trees" and "no natural shelter" emphasises the island's exposure and vulnerability

"Flung spray" suggests aggression, reinforcing the storm's violence

Sudden contrast between "company" in line 12 and "exploding" in line 13 is indicative of how the sea may at first seem gentle, but its true nature is violent

Simile reminds us the storm is unpredictable and uncontrollable, like a domestic animal suddenly turning wild

A simple, calm response to wild weather; also underscores a quiet respect for nature's power and a willingness to just wait it out instead of fight it

Oxymoronic "exploding comfortably" suggests the sea is powerful yet rhythmic and familiar to the community

Metaphor suggests emptiness itself is a weapon (salvo = multiple artillery rounds fired in quick succession), heightening the menacing, all-consuming threat of the storm

The wind "dives" and "strafes" like an air raid or military manoeuvre, attacking without warning to terrify an enemy force

"Bombarded" furthers the war imagery, redolent of withstanding an air raid, especially combined with the declaration that "we just sit tight" which depicts the community as resilient and resolute

Paradoxical "huge nothing" suggests fear is rooted in something intangible rather than a visible threat; this could also refer to a fear of mortality and the prospect of death being a huge nothingness

The tautology of "empty air" (when air is normally empty already) further emphasises barrenness and harshness of the natural environment whilst also creating haunting imagery of being bombarded by an invisible, unknowable force that threatens to overpower the community

"Strange" introduces uncertainty, suggesting the poem is about more than just nature – it may reflect existential fear or political conflict (i.e. The Troubles in Northern Ireland).

Theme key

- orange = community
- pink = control and strength
- green = nature
- blue = fear of the unknown

‘Tissue’ by Imtiaz Dharker

Key information

- **Poet:** Imtiaz Dharker (1954–)
- **Year:** 2006
- **Form:** Free verse
- **Key techniques:** Extended metaphor, symbolism, enjambment

About the poet

Imtiaz Dharker is a British-Pakistani poet and artist born in Lahore, raised in Glasgow, and settled in London. Her multicultural background deeply influences her poetry and her common focal points of belonging, borders, and the intersections of cultures. She has published several collections, many of which are accompanied by her own illustrations. Her poetic and documentary works frequently challenge societal norms, especially regarding gender, religion, and power structures.

Historical context

This is a contemporary poem from the 2000s, responding to the era's materialism and reliance on existing power structures. The references to religious texts and records of births and deaths acknowledges the long historical practice of documenting human existence on paper, highlighting its significance in preserving cultural identity.

Literary context

‘Tissue’ is part of Dharker's collection *The Terrorist at My Table* which explores themes of identity, power, and the transience of human life. The poem aligns with postmodern poetry by challenging rigid structures and emphasising impermanence and spirituality. Dharker's work also often engages with contemporary concerns about globalisation and human connections, which are evident in this poem's motifs of maps, money, and architecture.

Summary

‘Tissue’ is a reflective poem that explores the significance of paper as both a physical and symbolic entity. The poem begins by highlighting the delicate nature of paper, describing how light shines through it and how it records human history, particularly in books and religious texts. The mention of names, dates, and personal details underscores the role of paper in preserving human identity and memory. However, as the poem progresses, Dharker contends that paper structures, such as maps, receipts, and even buildings, are impermanent and subject to change. She contrasts the supposed strength of human constructions with their inevitable fragility, suggesting that even powerful institutions and borders are temporary. The poem presents a vision of an ideal world where structures are fluid and open, allowing for adaptability rather than rigid permanence. In the final lines, Dharker compares paper to human skin, emphasising the connection between the written word and human life. This metaphor reinforces the poem's central message: that despite our desire for permanence, everything, whether physical or conceptual, is ultimately ephemeral.

Key ideas

- Feelings of powerlessness
- Fragility vs. permanence
- The power of human connection
- Critiquing existing power structures
- Passage of time

Paper that lets the light
shine through, this
is what could alter things.
Paper thinned by age or touching,
the kind you find in well-used books,
the back of the Koran, where a hand
has written in the names and histories,
who was born to whom,
the height and weight, who
died where and how, on which sepia date,
pages smoothed and stroked and turned
transparent with attention.
If buildings were paper, I might
feel their drift, see how easily
they fall away on a sigh, a shift
in the direction of the wind.
Maps too. The sun shines through
their borderlines, the marks
that rivers make, roads,
railtracks, mountainfolds,

Fine slips from grocery shops
that say how much was sold
and what was paid by credit card
might fly our lives like paper kites.
An architect could use all this,
place layer over layer, luminous
script over numbers over line,
and never wish to build again with brick
or block, but let the daylight break
through capitals and monoliths,
through the shapes that pride can make,
find a way to trace a grand design
with living tissue, raise a structure
never meant to last,
of paper smoothed and stroked
and thinned to be transparent,
turned into your skin.

Paper is portrayed as something fragile yet transformative, taking this quotidian object and bestowing it with deep symbolism and the power to "alter things" for the better

Suggests enlightenment, optimism, and transparency

The continuous flow of lines mimics the softness and flexibility of paper

Thinning of paper conveys fragility and the passage of time

Everyday receipts are compared to profound aspects of life, highlighting consumerism's control over modern life

On the surface symbolise freedom, but in this context take on a sense of instability or even manipulation – our lives are controlled by financial records

The Koran is a sacred text, emphasising the reverence given to paper in serving as a record of faith and history

Metonymy of the hand represents the intimate human connection to paper

The extended metaphor of an architect, traditionally a builder of solid structures, now constructs using paper, implying a shift from materialism to a more ephemeral, artistic vision

Listing and repetition reinforces the idea that paper records important details that are intrinsic to human life and memory: birth, death, and relationships

Suggests knowledge, enlightenment, and an appreciation for what is delicate rather than rigid

Enjambment of "who / died" and the juxtaposition of the permanency of death with more mundane and changeable records of height and weight highlights the power of paper to capture the entire gamut of life

Symbols of power and permanence are juxtaposed with the idea of light breaking through, symbolising transparency and impermanence

Evocative of old photographs or faded ink, linking paper to the past and human memories

"Smoothed" and "stroked" evoke a tactile sense of handling delicate, precious documents, while "transparent with attention" suggest the paper is exposed and fragile from being handled, but also that they are clear and obvious, unlike more complex human constructs

This is where the poem most explicitly criticises the arrogance of human constructs – buildings, nations, and borders – suggesting they should be transparent and open to change

"Living tissue" connects paper with human skin, reinforcing the theme of vulnerability and impermanence; "Raise a structure" suggests ambition, yet it is "never meant to last," highlighting the transient nature of life and human achievements

The poem closes with a powerful transformation: paper becomes skin, suggesting deep personal history inscribed on the body. Skin is the barrier between our internal and external experiences, reinforcing the idea that history, knowledge, and memory are intrinsic to who we are

Imagery of the sun shining through borders suggests that national divisions are fragile and ultimately insignificant in the grand scheme of nature

Abrupt, short sentence and caesura interrupts flow and mimics the way maps divide territories and people

Use of hypothetical challenges the permanence of human-made structures, and the personification of them "sigh[ing]" makes them seem as light as breath in contrast to their usual solidity

Juxtaposition of natural formations with artificial ones, perhaps encouraging readers to question the permanence of human boundaries

Theme key

- Red = impermanence
- Pink = motif of light
- Green = paper symbolism
- Blue = human constructs

‘War Photographer’ by Carole Ann Duffy

Key information

- **Poet:** Carole Ann Duffy (1955–)
- **Year:** 1985
- **Form:** 4 stanzas, ABBCDD rhyme scheme
- **Key techniques:** Vivid imagery, juxtaposition, religious allusions

About the poet

Carol Ann Duffy was born in Glasgow and studied philosophy at the University of Liverpool, publishing her first book of poetry while still in university. In 2009, she became the first female Poet Laureate of the United Kingdom, a role she held until 2019. Her writing is widely acclaimed for its sharp wit, emotional depth, and ability to give voice to overlooked figures in history and everyday life. She has also written plays and children’s literature, and has been an outspoken advocate for literature and education, including the accessibility of poetry.

Historical context

In the 1980s, photojournalism played a crucial role in exposing the horrors of war. Conflicts such as the Vietnam War, the Troubles in Northern Ireland, and the Cambodian genocide had been widely documented, bringing the brutality of war into people’s homes through newspapers and television. The poem reflects on the emotional toll war photography takes on those who capture these images, contrasting their experiences with the detachment of their audience at a distance.

Literary context

The poem is part of Duffy’s 1985 collection *Standing Female Nude*, which explores themes of suffering, memory, and societal indifference. Duffy is known for her use of dramatic monologue and vivid imagery to give voice to marginalised or overlooked figures. ‘War Photographer’ follows this tradition, presenting the inner conflict of a photographer torn between his duty to document war and the emotional weight of witnessing human suffering.

Summary

‘War Photographer’ explores the psychological and moral dilemmas faced by a war photographer as he develops his images in a darkroom. The poem follows his reflections on the horrors he has witnessed in conflict zones such as Belfast, Beirut, and Phnom Penh. As he processes the photographs, he grapples with the emotional detachment required for his job and the delayed impact of trauma, which only surfaces when he is back home in England. The poem contrasts the war photographer’s memories of violence and suffering with the comfort and ignorance of those who view his photographs from the safety of their homes. The phrase “a hundred agonies in black and white” emphasises the stark reality of war, yet only a few images are selected for publication, reducing immense suffering to consumable media. The final lines of the poem highlight the disconnect between the photographer’s work and the audience’s fleeting empathy, as readers quickly move on from the horrifying images.

Key ideas

- Feelings of powerlessness
- Culpability and moral responsibility
- Reality of war
- Emotional distance from conflict
- Psychological consequences of war

Annotations

In his dark room he is finally alone
with spools of suffering set out in ordered rows.
The only light is red and softly glows,
as though this were a church and he
a priest preparing to intone a Mass.
Belfast. Beirut. Phnom Penh. All flesh is grass.

He has a job to do. Solutions slop in trays
beneath his hands, which did not tremble then
though seem to now. Rural England. Home again
to ordinary pain which simple weather can dispel,
to fields which don't explode beneath the feet
of running children in a nightmare heat.

Something is happening. A stranger's features
faintly start to twist before his eyes,
a half-formed ghost. He remembers the cries
of this man's wife, how he sought approval
without words to do what someone must
and how the blood stained into foreign dust.

A hundred agonies in black and white
from which his editor will pick out five or six
for Sunday's supplement. The reader's eyeballs prick
with tears between the bath and pre-lunch beers.
From the aeroplane he stares impassively at where
he earns his living and they do not care.

Opening characterised by isolation; "dark room" has a double meaning as a place to develop photographs and a metaphor for his psychological state

Contrasts the harsh realities of war with the calm of the darkroom

Suggests an attempt to impose structure on the chaos of war

Religious simile/metaphor compares the darkroom to a sacred space, reinforcing the photographer's reverence for his work. The suggestion that he is a priest performing a solemn duty implies he sees his work as an act of bearing witness to suffering

Powerful metaphor that sounds almost hypnotic but describes the photographic film containing images of pain and death

Red light is associated with darkrooms and photography, but also evokes connotations of danger, blood, and violence

The biblical reference (from Isaiah 40:6) reminds us of mortality and the transient nature of human life

Listing of war zones spans different continents and conflicts, emphasising the universality of human suffering; the abruptness of the place names also mimics the impersonal way war is reported

Sibilance and onomatopoeia to create a sense of movement and messiness; "solutions" also carries a double meaning: the chemical solutions used in developing film and potential solutions to war (which remain elusive)

Blunt statement detaches emotion from the work, emphasising duty over feeling

Lack of trembling "then" implies that while taking the photographs, he was composed or perhaps numbed by adrenaline, compared to now when he does tremble having to confront visual proof of the horrors of war

Diminishes trivial struggles of normal life

Imagery of explosions and invocation of the famous Vietnam War photograph of a child running from napalm attacks captures the literal heat of war as well as the metaphorical nightmare of suffering

Builds suspense and suggests the ghostly emergence of an image in the developing process; "A stranger's features" reinforces the anonymity of the victims he photographs

Suggests both the physical distortion and unfinished nature of the photograph and the haunting agony of war victims

The personal memory intrudes, showing how the photographer was not just an observer but engaged with the people he photographed

"Blood stained" is a stark image of violence, while "foreign dust" highlights both distance and disposability – life is lost in unfamiliar lands, forgotten by those far away, foreshadowing the poem's end

Metaphor for the oversimplification of war into digestible images, as well as the undeniable realities of suffering

Reduction of suffering to just a handful of images (and the cavalier idea of it being "five or six" as though one extra image could be an afterthought) highlights the selective and commercial nature of news reporting

Implies a fleeting, surface-level emotional response, not the deep empathy all people deserve

Juxtaposition of "tears" with mundane activities highlights the reader's detachment from real suffering. The rhyme between "tears" and "beers" further reinforces the trivialisation of war and people's flippant attitudes towards the suffering of others

The photographer is now distant again, both physically and emotionally; "impassively" suggests numbness, exhaustion, or resignation

Final line is stark and ambiguous: "they" could refer to the readers, the editor, or society as a whole. The blunt, detached tone leaves the poem on a pessimistic note, critiquing the indifference of the world toward war

Theme key

- red = war
- pink = moral responsibility
- green = suffering
- blue = response to trauma

Key ideas to compare between poems

	Conflict of war	Suffering and sacrifice	Power of nature	The powerful vs. the powerless	Strength vs. fragility	Trauma in response to conflict	Power of fear	Guilt vs. innocence	Power of memory	Loss of identity	Futility of conflict	Power of place and disposession
Bayonet Charge	✓	✓	✓			✓	✓			✓	✓	
The Charge of the Light Brigade	✓	✓		✓			✓	✓	✓	✓	✓	
Checking Out Me History		✓		✓	✓				✓			
The Émigrée		✓		✓	✓	✓			✓	✓		✓
Exposure	✓	✓	✓	✓	✓	✓	✓		✓	✓	✓	
Kamikaze	✓	✓	✓		✓	✓	✓	✓	✓	✓	✓	
London		✓		✓						✓		✓
My Last Duchess		✓		✓	✓		✓	✓	✓	✓		
Ozymandias	✓		✓	✓	✓				✓	✓	✓	
Poppies	✓	✓			✓	✓			✓		✓	✓
The Prelude			✓				✓		✓			✓
Remains	✓	✓		✓		✓	✓	✓	✓	✓		
Storm on the Island		✓	✓		✓		✓		✓			✓
Tissue			✓		✓				✓	✓		✓
War Photographer	✓	✓		✓	✓	✓	✓	✓	✓	✓	✓	